Our Daily Bread

Mary Quick

AuthorHouse™
1663 Liberty Drive
Bloomington, IN 47403
www.authorhouse.com
Phone: 1-800-839-8640

Published by AuthorHouse   11/11/2014

ISBN: 978-1-4969-5098-7 (sc)
978-1-4969-5097-0 (e)

Library of Congress Control Number: 2014919679

This book is printed on acid-free paper.

authorHOUSE®

Our Daily Bread

Mary Quick

Our Father which art in Heaven
Hallowed by thy name,

Padre nuestro Que estas en los
cielos Santificado sea tu nombre,

**Thy kingdom come.
Thy will be done on Earth,
as it is in Heaven.**

Venga a nosotros tu reino
Asi en el cielo com en la tierra.

Give us this day our daily bread and forgive us our debts, as we forgive our debtors.

El pan nuestro de cada dia, danosio hoy y perdonanos nuestras afensas,

**And lead us not into temptation,
but deliver us from evil.**

Asi como nosotros perdonamos
a los q nos afenden.

Perdonanos nustros pecados
y libranos de todo mal.

For thine is the kingdom, and the power, and the glory forever, Amen.

Ya que el reino, el poder y la Gloria son tuyos, por siempre, Amen.

Elder Mary Quick is a passionate woman who loves the Lord. She is the President of Healing & Restoration, a non-profit organization for women. She is also the owner of Faith's Maid Service of Thomasville, NC. Called by God to spread the gospel, Elder Quick is an ordained minister with the Ministry of Fullness Word of Faith, Inc. under the leadership of Pastor Olivia Allen. She has already written and published her autobiography, The Overcomer From Past to Present. Elder Quick resides in North Carolina with her husband and family.

Printed in the United States
By Bookmasters